CONTENTS

HOW TO USE THIS WORKBOOK   4

LIFE AND CAREER REFLECTION   5

RETIREMENT VISION   9

RETIREMENT DECISION   10

WHO YOU ARE   13

WHAT YOU DO   17
Meaningful Activities   17
Challenging Activities   18
Impact and Legacy   19

WHO IS INVOLVED   20
A Family Transition   22

HOW YOU STRUCTURE IT   23

REVISITING YOUR VISION FOR RETIREMENT   24

HOW TO USE THIS WORKBOOK

This workbook is intended to complement the book, *Retirement Life Plan: Navigating the transition from a rewarding career*, to further help you generate ideas, clarify possibilities, and identify specific action items for a smooth transition to a fulfilling life in retirement.

Retirement preparation—both financial and life planning—is linked with more positive outcomes in retirement. If you have not yet discussed your retirement plans with a professional financial advisor, it is strongly recommended that you do so; this plays a central role in determining your options for retirement. This workbook will then help you further clarify your vision for life in retirement.

What does a retirement life plan look like?

A life plan for retirement may look quite different from other plans—it may be much more flexible, fluid, and changing. That flexibility is, after all, one of the main benefits of retirement. The most important point is to develop a realistic vision and generate ideas that fit your personal circumstances and preferences. Whether you prefer to create a detailed agenda for retirement, or explore a range of possibilities, giving serious consideration to life in retirement is the first step to a smooth and positive transition.

This workbook starts with a *life and career reflection*, as this forms the foundation for your retirement transition. You will then explore your general *vision for retirement*—what you hope retirement will look like. If you are still wrestling with whether or not to retire, you may also explore the section on the retirement decision. The subsequent sections will then help you take a deeper dive into different aspects of retirement, namely your *identity (Who you are)*, *social networks and relationships (Who is involved)*, *activities and pursuits (What you do)*, and *structuring free time* (How you structure it). Retirement experiences vary considerably from person to person, so some sections may seem more relevant than others. However, I encourage you to consider each area.

LIFE AND CAREER REFLECTION

With the prospect of retirement, many people simply look ahead, without taking time to reflect on previous experiences and chapters in life. Your personal stories in life and in your career form the foundation for your transition to retirement. These may impact your current attitude toward retirement, your decision to retire, and, of course, your experiences with retirement. Reflecting on your life experiences will provide some insight for the direction you would like to take in retirement.

CAREER REFLECTION:

What have been some of the most satisfying points in your career? What was it about these points that you found satisfying? What were you doing at the time? Who else was involved?

_____

_____

_____

_____

_____

_____

_____

_____

_____

_____

_____

_____

_____

_____

_____

_____

_____

_____

_____

_____

_____

_____

What have you found most rewarding in your career? What accomplishments are you most proud of? What challenges did you overcome, and what lessons did you learn?

_____

_____

_____

_____

_____

_____

_____

_____

_____

_____

_____

What relationships did you develop in your career? What relationships have expanded into friendships outside of the workplace? What common interests do you share with these friends?

_____

_____

_____

_____

_____

_____

_____

_____

_____

_____

_____

_____

LIFE SATISFACTION:

These reflections may overlap with reflections on your career, as experiences in one area tend to impact other areas.

What have been some of the most satisfying points in your life as a whole?
What was it about these points that you found satisfying? What were you doing at the time?
Who else was involved?

_____

_____

_____

_____

_____

_____

_____

_____

_____

_____

_____

_____

_____

_____

_____

_____

_____

_____

_____

_____

_____

_____

_____

_____

What have you found most rewarding in your life as a whole? What accomplishments are you most proud of? What challenges did you overcome, and what lessons did you learn?

_____

_____

_____

_____

_____

_____

_____

What relationships have you developed outside of work?
What relationships have been an important part of your life outside of work?

_____

_____

_____

_____

_____

_____

_____

_____

_____

RETIREMENT VISION

Everyone has a different vision for retirement - whether it involves continuing some form of work, more time with family, slowing down to appreciate life, or more time for personal pursuits. Retirement takes on many forms, and no one lifestyle will suit everyone.

As you approach retirement, others might offer advice on how to spend your time. It is important, however, to step back and reflect on your own personal vision for this next chapter in life, perhaps with the same consideration as you most likely gave to your career. This will help you design a retirement life that will provide personal fulfillment.

What does retirement mean to you?
What are the first words or phrases that come to mind when you think of retirement?

_____

_____

_____

_____

_____

What is your ideal vision for retirement?
What will you be doing? Who else will be involved? How will you feel?

_____

_____

_____

_____

_____

_____

Does your vision reflect involvements for the short-term, long-term, or both?

_____

_____

_____

_____

People often imagine things like travel, fixing up the house, and relaxation as central to their retirement. However, these pursuits tend to be short-lived; once they are finished, you are left wondering, now what? Consider some regular activities and hobbies that may be continued through the first few years of retirement, after pursuits such as travel and relaxation.

RETIREMENT DECISION

The retirement decision is largely a financial matter; however, other factors also tend to play a significant role in the process. For instance, the timing of a partner's retirement, employment circumstances, or attitudes toward retirement may all contribute to a feeling of being pushed or pulled toward retirement—or toward continued work. Writing down the pros and cons of retirement, and the factors pushing or pulling you, in either direction, may help to clarify things.

List the pros and cons you imagine with retirement versus continued work.

	PROS	CONS
RETIREMENT		
CONTINUED WORK		

Retirement usually involves a mix of factors that push or pull you in either direction. Push factors are those things making you feel that you should (or have to) retire/ continue work. Pull factors are those things that attract you to the idea of retirement/ continued work. Identifying these factors may help to clarify any mixed emotions around retirement.

List the factors you feel are:

- pushing you to retire
- pulling (or drawing you) toward retirement
- pushing you to continue work
- pulling (or drawing you) toward continued work

	RETIREMENT	CONTIDUE(D) WORK
PUSHING ME TO		
PULLING / DRAWING ME TOWARD		

Retirement tends to have either highly positive or negative associations (e.g., travel and relaxation versus declining health and boredom). Neither of these extremes is a very accurate representation of most retirees' experiences. However, attitudes toward retirement play a central role in the retirement decision, as well as the adjustment experience.

Fears and uncertainties may contribute to unnecessary stress and anxiety, or simply cause one to put off retirement. It's important to address and challenge any fears you have about retirement. Reframe your thinking about retirement with your own, personalized definition of this chapter in life. Along with this workbook, the book, *Retirement Life Plan: Navigating the transition from a rewarding career*, will help in developing a more balanced, and personalized view of retirement.

What fears or uncertainties do you have about retirement, if any?
You may refer back to the previous section, Retirement Vision, and consider the first words and phrases that came to mind with retirement. Do these reflect any concerns about retirement?

_____

_____

_____

_____

_____

Reframe retirement.
If you were to develop your own definition for retirement, what would it be?

_____

_____

_____

_____

_____

WHO YOU ARE

The first question we are usually asked when meeting a new person is, *what do you do*? This underscores the way in which our work shapes how others see us, as well as how we see ourselves. Work often becomes integrated with our sense of self; because of this, identity adjustments may be a significant part of your retirement transition.

Ideally, your identity will form a central part of your retirement vision. Your involvements are more likely to be experienced as meaningful and engaging when they align with your personal values and interests. So before brainstorming a bucket list of things to do in retirement, or social groups to join, consider your top personal values, interests, and priorities in this phase of life.

The life and career reflection, earlier in this workbook, also forms part of your personal story, which becomes integrated with your sense of self. Reflecting back on these personal stories may help to inform your journey to retirement, and perhaps areas that you may want to focus on in your transition—e.g., the most enjoyable points in your career and life as a whole may shed light on possible pursuits for retirement.

Tell your personal story, from career to retirement.

If our personal stories form an important part of our sense of self, you may want to consider how retirement fits into your personal story. Referring back to reflections earlier in this workbook, write (or tell a friend) the story of both your career and your upcoming retirement, and what it means to you.

Take stock of your personal values and priorities:
List seven things that are most important to you now, at this point in your life. Then, looking ahead to retirement, list seven things that you imagine will be most important to you in retirement.

You might consider different areas of life, such as leisure, health, relationships, finances, spirituality, personal development, etc. Personal values and priorities often shift and change around the time of retirement; make note of any differences in your priorities as you look ahead to retirement.

TOP PRIORITIES NOW (IN YOUR CAREER)	TOP PRIORITIES IN RETIREMENT
1.	
2.	
3.	
4.	
5.	
6.	
7.	

Take stock of your personal interests:
List seven things that you find most interesting, engaging, or enjoyable in your work and/or life outside of work.

1.
2.
3.
4.
5.
6.
7.

What aspects of work do you connect with most, and what does this mean for retirement? How might you continue with these aspects of work after retirement? For instance, if you enjoyed leading teams, analyzing data, or helping colleagues, what retirement pursuits may be of a similar quality?

_____

_____

_____

_____

_____

_____

_____

_____

Keeping busy and filling your days might ward off feelings of boredom; but you will probably find it more fulfilling to focus on just a few activities that you find positive, meaningful, and rewarding.

MEANINGFUL ACTIVITIES

Meaningful activities bring about benefits to health, happiness, and the ability to cope with adversities. They also contribute to a more general sense of meaning in life. *So what exactly are meaningful activities?*

Activities that align with your personal values, interests, and goals are more likely to be experienced as meaningful, important, and worthwhile. So while others might recommend pursuits that they have found meaningful, these may be quite different from what you will experience as meaningful. Start with your personal values and interests, then brainstorm potentially meaningful retirement pursuits.

Brainstorm meaningful pursuits:
List some of your top personal interests, values, and priorities from the previous section (Who You Are). Then, brainstorm specific activities or pursuits that align with these. For instance, if improving health is a top priority, you might list ideas such as yoga, cycling, or taking a cooking class to encourage healthy eating at home.

TOP PERSONAL INTERESTS, PRIORITIES, AND VALUES	RELATED ACTIVITIES AND PURSUITS
1.	
2.	
3.	
4.	
5.	
6.	
7.	

CHALLENGING ACTIVITIES

Often times, work is where you will encounter a lot of new and unique challenges and problems to solve. These may be a source of stress; at the same time, however, they often contribute to feelings of mastery, personal control, and a sense of reward and accomplishment.

Problem solving opportunities are generally not as prevalent in retirement as they are with work. You may find that some part-time work or unpaid volunteer work is the right fit for you, providing some challenges and sense of accomplishment. However, you can also look to some of your personal interests and leisure pursuits to provide a challenge. This will mean actively finding new ways to stretch yourself in those personal pursuits.

What possible retirement activities will involve the pursuit of success, accomplishment, or mastery? Consider activities you already enjoy outside of work, as well as new pursuits.

_____

_____

_____

_____

What new skills and abilities would you like to develop in retirement?

_____

_____

_____

What skills or abilities do you already have, that you would like to push to the next level and develop further?

_____

_____

_____

How could you build and develop these new and existing skills?

_____

_____

_____

_____

IMPACT AND LEGACY

Activities that involve being productive, making a contribution to something bigger than oneself, or having an impact on others are likely to support feelings of self-esteem and usefulness in retirement. Generativity—contributing to younger generations—has also been identified as an important part of adult development in the later years. The idea of leaving a legacy may also fall into this category. As you approach retirement, consider the ways in which you would like to have an impact, or leave your mark in the world—however big or small.

What kind of impact would you like to have in retirement? What kind of mark would you like to leave on others, or the world? For ideas and inspiration, try referring back to your priorities and interests.

_____

_____

_____

_____

_____

_____

_____

_____

_____

_____

WHO IS INVOLVED

Positive and healthy relationships play a critical role in health and wellbeing throughout our lifespan. They enhance our feelings of self-worth, and even have a positive impact on our physical health. This is particularly relevant for retirement, as it represents a very different phase of life with regard to our social lives.

Retirement frees us from the very structured work environments in which we are often obligated to interact and deal with others, even when we would rather not. It also means leaving behind many of the positive interactions enjoyed through work, and perhaps a primary source of social involvement.

Maintaining an active social life is a responsibility that falls on your shoulders once you retire. For some, this is no problem. For those who have relied on work as a social outlet, however, it may spell trouble. If you are someone who prefers to keep yourself, this section is also particularly important for you—we are all social creatures and need some amount of social interaction for our emotional, cognitive, and physical health.

Who do you currently socialize with outside of work?
List specific friends or groups, as well as acquaintances, places, or activities where you tend to interact with others.

> *Your current social network, outside of work, will form the foundation for your social interactions in retirement. "Taking stock" of your relationships outside of work will give you a sense for what your social environment will be like in retirement, and perhaps whether you should begin expanding your social network.*

Which of these relationships are positive and supportive?
Of the relationships you listed above, note those that leave you feeling positive or energized. Of those that are not so enjoyable, consider possibilities for scaling back your time and commitment to the relationship.

_____

_____

_____

_____

_____

_____

Identify five possible social outlets in retirement.
Referring back to your personal values and interests, identify five people, groups, or social gatherings that align with your values and interests. You might also search online to identify relevant groups related to your interests

TOP PERSONAL INTERESTS, PRIORITIES, AND VALUES	RELATED SOCIAL GROUPS AND ACTIVITIES
1. _____	_____
2. _____	_____
3. _____	_____
4. _____	_____
5. _____	_____

Commit to regular social activities.
It's not always easy joining new social groups. If you're someone who enjoys spending time alone, it may be particularly important to commit to a few regular social engagements in retirement. Remember, you will grow more comfortable with a new group after a few meetings. You may also need to test out different groups before finding one that suits you.

List three social groups that you will commit to joining in retirement.

1. _____

2. _____

3. _____

A FAMILY TRANSITION

Retirement is not only a transition for the retiree—it's a family transition. It may be a perfect opportunity to focus more on family; however, it may also involve adjustments for everyone involved. Couples report having to make adjustments with regard to sharing space around the house, negotiating household responsibilities, and managing their time spent together versus separately. The adjustment experience also tends to differ depending on whether couples retiree together, or at different times.

Either way, couples find that the key to successfully managing this change is to keep communication open throughout the process: from pre-retirement planning to post-retirement adjustment. It's crucial to continue talking openly about your hopes, expectations, and experiences with family members.

Communicate expectations with family members.
Make a point to share your retirement vision and expectations with your spouse, children, and any other close family members who may be impacted. Also find out about their own expectations regarding your retirement, and how they think it may impact them.

Who have you already discussed your retirement plans with? Who else will you discuss your plans with?

_____

_____

_____

_____

Identify activities that you will enjoy pursuing along with your spouse, and those you will pursue independently. Balancing time together versus apart can be a critical part of retirement adjustment for couples. Consider how you will manage this balance and openly discuss these ideas with your spouse.

SHARED PURSUITS	INDEPENDENT PURSUITS

An abundance of free time is one of the most highly anticipated benefits of retirement. We anxiously await the freedom from overly rigid and demanding schedules, and the ability to do what we want, when we want. Ironically, however, an abundance of unstructured free time may also be problematic. Some retirees struggle with a lack of motivation or sense of purpose for the day. Without routine or external obligations, they may report feelings of aimlessness, difficulty starting projects, or feeling that there is a void in their lives.

Others struggle with the opposite problem, feeling bombarded and overwhelmed with external demands on their time. These retirees find that some time management is actually needed in order to handle the requests coming in from others, and to maintain time for themselves.

A balance between an overly structured routine and an abundance of unstructured free time is optimal. In fact, free time management has been linked to greater quality of life in retirement. How this is implemented will of course vary from person to person—some prefer more structure than others. Developing a new rhythm and (still flexible) routine in retirement is not meant to constrain you, but to help you achieve your plans for retirement.

What activities will you be involved in on a regular basis? Examples might include meeting friends for coffee once a week, morning walks, or caring for grandchildren once a week.

_____

_____

_____

Ideally, what might a typical day look like in retirement? For instance, how will you start your days? What sort of activities might you do throughout the day?

_____

_____

_____

_____

_____

_____

_____

_____

_____

REVISITING YOUR VISION FOR RETIREMENT

After reflecting on various aspects of retirement life, take a moment to revisit your vision for retirement.

What does retirement mean to you? How do you envision life in retirement? What do you imagine doing (e.g., what will be some of your regular pursuits)? Who else will be involved (e.g., what social groups will you be a part of)? How do you imagine retirement will feel?

_____

_____

_____

_____

_____

_____

_____

_____

_____

_____

_____

_____

_____

_____

_____

_____

_____

_____

_____

Action Items: Finally, based on your reflections in this workbook, identify two specific actions you will take now, to help you prepare for this transition to retirement. For instance, if you came up with ideas for new pursuits or social activities, what specific actions might you take now to start your involvement in these?

1. _____

2. _____

Made in the USA
Monee, IL
19 July 2021